Maggie Caldwell

Bird Notes from the Mountains

Maggie Caldwell

Bird Notes from the Mountains

ISBN/EAN: 9783337317423

Printed in Europe, USA, Canada, Australia, Japan

Cover: Foto ©Andreas Hilbeck / pixelio.de

More available books at **www.hansebooks.com**

=:= BIRD NOTES =:=

==from the==

∴ MOUNTAINS. ∴

POEMS

–BY–

MAGGIE CALDWELL.

LEBANON, VA.:
E. K. HARDING, PUBLISHER.
1888.

INTRODUCTION.

——::——

THIS Introduction has caused me more annoyance and more discomfiture than the writing of this little volume of poems. How to apologize for something that I am not yet sorry to have written,—how to make pleas for what I did not attempt to refrain from doing,—how to excuse what I could not help but do, are tasks beyond my feeble strength.

So, dear reader. I shall send my little book out in the world to fight its own battles as best it may, and only beg that you will be lenient with such a frail voyager. The dreaded reefs will be reached soon enough, where many thousands better than my work, have been engulfed in oblivion. But while the sunlight sparkles on the wave. and all seems fair, seek not to impede its course.

Whether this work will benefit or give any great pleasure is doubtful. as I claim for it no great merit. it being the productions of a yet undeveloped and untrained mind.

I hold it nothing more than the mere beginning of a life-labor, whose future may blush to own the present.

Why I wrote these poems. or how the idea was conceived to give vent to my thoughts in verse are mysteries to me.

If any honor should attend the publication of this collection I claim none for myself. but gladly give it where it rightfully belongs—to Hollins Institute.

It is to my Alma Mater that I am due any inspiration that may have led to these productions. And if any dreams of beauty are brought to the mind of the kind reader. or whispered word of strange creeds, the thought was born beneath the rugged brow of

—

Tinker Mountain which overlooks the dearest Alma Mater our Southern girls could claim.

Beneath the quiet shades of this college. where every breeze seemed to whisper a poem I wrote most of these pieces.

I did not dream then that they would ever be read by my friends with any degree of pleasure. but thought only of the. exquisite joy it gave myself to exist in a world peopled with beings of my own imagination.

My deepest regret is that my work is not more worthy of him to whom I dedicate it, and of my Alma Mater.

My apology should be why I ever had these poems published in the present form: Partly because I was vain enough to wish to see my own name attached to a book as its author; and partly. for "all was not vanity" I assure you. because it was the desire of many of my friends that I should do so.

Go, little book. and if you should give your readers one thousandth part of the pleasure that you have afforded your humble writer in composing you, all her labors will be amply repaid.

THE AUTHORESS.

NEW GARDEN. VA..
Dec. 3. 1887.

BIRD NOTES

from the

MOUNTAINS.

LINES.

I pressed my lips to Nature's cup,
  And tried to drink with a single sup
So greedy and mad, the contents up,
  And drain to the bottom the very cup.

My lips had scarcely touched the brim,
  When fast before me it began to swim,
And all at once it grew so dim
  I failed to see even the rim.

O, Mother Nature! I cried aloud,
  My heart I 'll bend though ever so proud;
No matter what to thee I 've vowed,
  Amid the changing, rushing crowd.

Come back and slake my burning lip!
  In your cool bosom Oh! let me dip,
Renew my life with a single sip,
  With only a drop on my finger tip.

She would not hear but turned away,
  And far o'er the hills she seemed to stray,
She kissed the sky with light like day,
  And left me to pine alway, alway.

A wild sad thought ran through my soul,
  And o'er my nerves a chill so cold,
That to me I seemed a century old,
  And my limbs had lost their action bold.

I flung my arms in wild despair,
  I tossed in frantic rage my hair,
But all that met my sternest stare
  Was darkness still, and nothing there.

The angel of night now marked my lair,
  Despair, my friend, who incensed my fear,
And shadows crept so near, so near,
  That in the gloom they seemed to appear.

So great my woe and anguish wild,
  My heart was numb and made so mild,
That I was humble as a little child,
  And my being to calmness beguiled.

My heart-strings I made into a poet's lute,
  And sang to make my fears all mute,
My anguish I need to try to confute,
  Nature's slight, and my woe compute.

Oh! listen friends to my wildest song!
  And if to you it should seem too long,
It is my woe so great and far prolonged,
  While a thousand sounds with it throng.

When life is done then will cease the string,
  My blighted hopes will cease to sing,
But to the fount of sorrow I 'll bring   [spring.
  My inmost thoughts, and from whence they

THE MOUNTAIN.

Old mountain dark and bare and hoary,
   Reveal to me your strange dark story!
I wish to know from whence you came,
   And what on earth has made your fame?

" Beneath the ocean was my home,
   But from my bed I was rudely torn,
With ocean shells upon my crest,
   And rugged rocks around my breast.

I pierced the calm and azure sky,
   And stood a lofty tower on high,
A landmark for the eyes of men
   On which to turn their wearied ken.

I've stood for ages just as now
   And turned to the sun the same dark brow,
Around my bosom and o'er my head
   The storm-clouds came and swiftly sped.

The iron comes from my dusky heart;
   Though all reluctant to let it part,
I love the bold inventions of man,
   And gladly give a helping hand.

The gold that glitters in the royal crown,
   Once in my bosom was firmly bound,
But brilliantly it shines on the royal head
   Of the proud young king whom ambition has fed.

The foot of the hunter has pressed my side
   As on to the prey, boldly he tried
My rugged steeps, his soul beat free,
   And his blood ran warm with joyous glee.

I nourish the patriot in my twilight glen,
    And teach him his soul to upward bend,
To climb the height of human joy,
    And in God's work his strength employ.

———:———

THE STORM.

The month was wild and stormy March,
    The hills were gray, and cold, and bare.
A storm from heaven's darkened arch,
    Was howling loud and with fury there.

The snow came down in the hurrying blast,
    And softly kissed the ground in glee;
It fell so silent, white and fast,
    That Heaven's emblem it seemed to be.

My thoughts were wandering far away
    Into the regions of the snow,
Into the land where every spray
    Is congealed by winds that blow.

When a note so wild, so sad, so drear,
    From out the limbs of an aged tree,
Soon roused me with a sigh and tear,
    That grief and suffering there could be.

A shivering bird sat on the limb,
    In the Sunny South a bird who sang
Her notes of joy; and carols that win
    Her mate in love, so sweetly rang.

But lured by one sunny day,
    And called by the voice of spring,
She came in our cold clime to stay
    And through the summer here to sing.

She fought the storm with frantic rage,
  And fluttered wild with all her might,
But she could not break the icy cage
  Which bound and stopped her upward flight.

A note of mingled grief and fear
  Attended every movement made,
She looked for refuge far and near,
  But all with snow was overlaid.

But cold and stiff her limbs now grew,
  And slowly she moved upon the tree,
And in her bosom all sound so true,
  Died away in death's silent sea.

Oh! ne'er, sweet bird, in your happiest home,
  Where song so thrilling, touching clear,
Though coming from your blissful bower,
  Where love and truth are united dear.

So thus it is in this short life,
  Too much we trust to one bright day,
And soon forgotten is the strife,
  Deceived, our thoughts glide far away.

Then life goes out not in a song
  As the notes of this wild bird,
But life to us becomes a wrong
  From which no joy is ever heard.

———:———

THE BRIDGE OF DESPAIR.

I stole from the city's restless motion,
  I sought some lonely place to think,
Away from the wretched human ocean,
  Which chilled my soul and made it shrink.

The great dark bridge that spans the river,
  The river that rolls in inky darkness.
I sought with a strange wild quiver,
  For ah! to me all was blackness.

The great iron bars that cross the flood
  Spoke of mighty strength and power.
And such must be the nerve and blood
  That conquers life or soon will cower.

The noble spirit of mortal man;
  For wide he stretches and looks afar,
And with a brief life tries to span,
  The space from earth to the fartherest star.

On an awful bridge I stood.
  The bridge that spans the river of life,
The waves reflected my sullen mood,
  And in my soul was sickening strife.

The waters seemed to speak to me.
  And whisper softly. "Here is rest.
What is life that you should be.
  Come and sleep upon my breast."

Every moment all grew darker.
  Dark as Charon's awful tide,
In my soul and on the water,
  Not a star shone as my guide.

With clenched hands I muttered low,
  Rest I 'll find. ah! silent river,
Rest from time's great pain and woe,
  Beneath your waves which never quiver.

With savage joy I sought the brink,
  And peered into the gloomy tide,
Oh! those waters that soon would link
  My wretched soul to Death's cold side.

From the inky waves a glorious light
  In sudden beauty and grandeur came,
The pale-faced moon so soft and bright
  From the water seemed to flame.

A silent star kept near her side
  And dimly shone through the falling rays,
To the silvery queen it seemed a guide,
  As glorious as the king who rules the days.

Each wave a wondrous brightness took,
  And flashed a brilliant, radiant gleam;
The iron bars a diamond nook
  With beauteous light now streamed.

O'er my soul the soft light shone,
  A quiet star came up in my heart,
From the door was rolled the stone,
  And dead hope came forth with a start.

From the water's edge I quickly passed,
  I walked the bridge with its mighty bars,
My nerves were steel, my steps were fast,
  My thoughts now with the radiant stars.

On every gloomy sea of woe,
  If you will wait a moon will rise,
And every wave will be aglow,
  With glorious light from upper skies.

TWO PATHS.

PART I.

The sun's last rays had tinged the hills with gold,
  The shadows dark were stealing o'er the world,
And nature kind with gentle touch and true,
  Was soothing all as she was want to do.

How sweet the evening's fragrant scent and breeze,
  At close of summer's day when from the trees,
A thousand little whirl-winds gayly play,
  Impart their mountain breath and hie on their way.

A sweeter gale had never stirred the leaf,
  Or told of mountain flower soft and brief,
As Clinch's verdant sides gave forth so true,
  To sweep the quiet vale of Mountain View.

Down through the vale a silver streamlet glides,
  Whose sparkling waters o'er pebbles sing, and sides
Are clothed in green, and modest touch-me-nots
  Drop their heads to conceal their crimson spots.

A rude and quaintly cottage covered wild
  With clambering rose, and vine kind nature's child,
Stood on the bank of the murmuring stream,
  Where song was as music heard only in a dream.

An aged tree his shadow dark had cast
  On the roof and sward, across the stream and past;
His leafy top was bathed in fiery light,
  As the sun so red sank slowly out of sight.

A bird sang soft from a limb, in the evening calm,
  And twittered to his mate of the heavenly balm
Of rest and sleep, as he sought his leafy home,
  To dream of morrow's flight and where to roam.

The cottagers with simple hearts and minds,   [binds
  Shut out from wisdom's page, which starves and
The soul. while drop by drop it yields and gives,
  Dwell here where love and sweet contentment live.

The aged sire with locks of snow, sat near,
  And watched his wife prepare the evening cheer;
A sturdy lad who oft his strength had tried
  In woodland sports, had sought the water's side.

A little girl of ten, his play-mate dear,
  With laughing eyes and sunny hair, crept near
To fright him with her unexpected coming,
  Aud pelt him with her flowers before his turning.

Ah! this was peaceful love and envied rest,
  Though meager fare provide the wants of breast,
Their hearts knew not of greater, statelier joy,
  But simple needs their minds and thoughts employ.

No burning. fiery passions kindle here,
  Ambition's love does not scorch and sear
The soul, but all in gentler, quiet peace
  Live, as if human strife had ceased.

The inquiry comes, "Will e'er in breast arise
  A thirst this stream can never slake, and cries
From a hungry soul burst forth, that never more
  Can be fed by your mountain dark and hoar?"

The wild desire that spurs the spirit on,
  Takes hold and burns till all feeling is gone,
Such lonely, heavenly spots loves to seek,
  Converting Eden into a night dark and bleak.

'Tis the simple, noble, truthful heart,
  On which ambition tries her deceiving art,
Her dupe must climb from the lowest rounds of life,
  And reach the top through every opposing strife.

PART II.

Autumn's chilling winds had come at last,
  And thickly the leaves were falling in each blast,
Covering the earth with the richest, brightest hues,
  While every hill and vale were gorgeous views.

The Autumn flower mingling with the leaf
  Relieved the heart of thoughts of woe and grief,
That everything was slowly, sadly dying,
  For nature is but a name for change and sighing.

The purple grape in luscious clusters gem
  Amid the fading trees of Mountain View,
And every rustling, quivering leaf that fell,
  A tale of gladness as well as grief could tell.

The mist had scarcely left the mountain top,
  The dew still sparkled on the forget-me-not,
The bird had scarcely left her quiet nest
  Where she the night before had found her rest.

When from the cottage door a youth came out,
  Who turned with restless, sadened brow about,
And looked around the home he thought to leave,
  For which he thought never after to grieve.

Upon his stalwart shoulders a knap-sack he bore,
  In which his simple clothes, the mountaineer's store,
From each of those he loved a simple gift
  He took to keep, no matter what would be his shift.

A few summers more had gently stamped his brow,
  Since last we saw him in the self-same place as now,
Sporting there with joyous, childish glee,
  From every harrowing care and woe so free.

But these short years had strangely changed the youth,
  A restles spirit, a longing wild for truth.
The rugged mountain peaks could bind no longer
  This rising soul which every day grew stronger.

He dreamed a world lay far beyond these peaks,
  Bright with thought and action, and he who seeks
To realize this dream, would surely gain
  Ambition's dazzling crown, for all his pain.

The aged man came forth with feeble step,
  And close beside his partner frail had kept,
Not far behind the bright-haired girl now came,
  But she, you well could tell, was still the same.

As this small group stood in the grayish dawn,
  While scarcely o'er the mount the sun yet shone,
The bright and brilliant scene drew not an eye,
  Though all was fair,—the earth, and trees, and sky.

Each heart was filled with the greatest human woe,
  Their anguish and pain, oh! who on earth can know!
The aged pair a noble son was losing,
  The little girl her only friend for amusing.

The old man spoke, "you are about to leave,
  For you, behind are friends who 'll sadly grieve;
You think to reach a lofty height in life,
  But you may fail, however great your strife.

Yonder lofty peak you've often scaled,
  And heard the chilling winds around it wail,
You 've noted well its barren, rugged top,
  Where blooms not even the lone forget-me-not.

Oh! thus is eminence in this poor world of ours,
  Though high we build our plans and Eden bowers;
Oh! listen, son, to what the aged say,
  Take warning now and with me stay, oh! stay."

"My father," sadly spoke the youth and sighed,
  "Why seek to save me from the ebbing tide?
My blood runs warm, my brain seems now on fire,
  Another field of action than this I desire.

I long to oppose and strive with other men,
  And crush them back, if need, to reach my end;
Here I'd pine away for action bold,
  Ambition would consume but ne'er grow cold.

Farewell, my father, forgive my greatest wrong;
  I did not think to grieve, for kindness long
To repay you thus, my best and kindest friend,
  And anguish to your aged heart to send."

He turned away and soon was lost to sight,
  But every eye had followed fast his flight;
He left his home a sad and lonely place.
  Near his parents joy no longer had a space.

PART III.

Time moves on; and in his dreaded course,
  He bears no joys, but all are sorrows hoarse,
Which smite our heart, and grate upon our ears,
  Decrease our pleasures and much increase our fears.

Time moves on; he leaves on every brow
  His foot-prints clear, which plainly tell us now,
That fast across our path the sorrows came,
  And these left us always not the same.

We watch each fading light along our life,
  We try to hold the sunbeam with eager strife,
But quickly through our hands it slips away,
  And only the shadows dark will with us stay.

And this has been the fate of the weary mother,
  Who dying lay, without kind friend or brother,
Though children that she had labored hard to raise,
  Gathered around her bed to weep and praise.

'Tis fifty years since she had said farewell
  To her brother, in the self-same mountain dell.
'Tis fifty years since heavy-hearted and sad,
  She had climbed the hill with vines all clad,

To weep alone for brother and play-mate dear,
  Who never more would come again or be near;
Her heart grew sad, even days could not allay
  The pain, and sorrow knew would always stay.

The girl no longer gathered grapes upon the hills,
  The flowers had lost their hues, the stream its trills,
And aimless from day to day she wandered about,
  The sunshine of her life had forever gone out.

But everything at length must have an end;
  To our greatest woes we cease to lend
Our hearts, and to our keenest joys we give
  Not even the thoughts that would make them live.

It was not years until she ceased to weep;   [sleep,
  Nor was it long until she woke from childhood's
A maiden fair she found her self already grown,
  And the seeds of a new life ready to be sown.

A youth not far above her own rude life,
  Came to woe and win her for his wife;
A higher path she could not hope to gain—
  She could not say him nay, and give him pain.

A new log cottage was placed beside the old,
  And proud the youthful husband looked, and bold,
As to this home he lead his bonny bride,
  Who never more would wish to leave his side.

Sweet and cheerily she sang at the spinning-wheel,
  Though tired, her face was bright at every meal,
For oft she gathered up the hoe and rake,
  And tilled the corn, and oft the hay would make.

A sweeter lullaby could not be heard at night,
　As she sang o'er her children soft and bright,
No shadow of labor lingered around that song,
　No tinge of passions which might lead her wrong.

Not many years she dwelt in peace and joy,
　While busily she worked and her time employed,
For death now took the aged, feeble pair,
　And quietly they passed to that upper world so fair.

But her greatest sorrow came when low she laid
　The husband of her youth, and silently prayed
To God to help her, in her double care,
　Where no friend was left her burden to share.

But fast her weary life was ebbing away,
　While shrill the wind was whistling this winter day;
With feeble motion the tattered quilt she tossed,
　And on her faded breast her hands she crossed.

She murmured something of her brother low,
　But ere her friends her only wish could know,
Her gentle spirit had passed to its God,
　And her face told plainly that near the angels trod.

They bore her to the hill all clad in vines,
　Which oft had rung to her childish glee and chimes,
And for her youthful pleasure had been the spot,
　And in her death this place was not forgot.

The sighing winds of winter wailing round,
　And the sob of friends were the only sounds
That followed this noble soul to the silent grave,
　But what other boon from friends should any crave!

PART IV.

A poet once dreamed that in the crowded street,
  Where thousands surge and not a friend to greet,
That human hearts would press our souls the most,
  And make us see the strong and weaker parts,

That lurk in human souls and make them fail,
  Or give them strength the strongest seas to sail,
A weakness all would like to learn of another,
  But in ourselves this fault we seek to smother.

It may be in the city's restless motion,
  Where surge and roll the greatest human ocean,
That victims more are seen and sifted,
  But faults the same exist among the hills uplifted.

It was in the old crowded quaker city,   [pity,
  Where thousands meet and pass without thought or
While driving sleet and snow were falling fast,
  And each with hurrying steps was hastening past,

That through the croud a man of noble form
  Now passed, and each gave back as though one born
Of noble race, had come to rule all men,
  And they before him the knee must humbly bend.

He passed with swifter steps than those who went,
  And scarcely felt the driving sleet, which spent
Its fury upon his snowy beard and brow,
  But touched not his face for wraps would not allow.

He quickly reached his grand and stately home,
  When there he found himself just all alone;
He flung aside his cold reserve and pride,
  And sought to relieve his heart so early tried.

Upon a couch with scarlet velvet lining,
  He flung him down with hearty groans and sighing;
The gas-light gleamed o'er marble stands, and busts
  From every nook peep out as if distrusts,

Had seized their icy forms and made them feel
  A heart was breaking whose texture was steel;
The richest rays from costly carpet came,
  But there was sadness even in the flame.

This man of iron-heart had pushed his way,
  Alone he stood in glory's eternal day,
He 'd climbed the top from the lowest round of fame,
  On the rock of high renown he 'd writ his name.

Heart-sick and sore on the dizzy height he stood,
  None to share his fame or calm his mood,
While high the wind was blowing this stormy night,
  He turned away aweary from grandeur's sight,

And sweetly dreamed of other days, so free
  From every care and woe, when bowed his knee
Beside a kind but humble mother's chair,
  While fast his hand was held by a sister fair.

He crossed the dell to find the cow at eve,
  He called her loud to hear the echoes cleave
And backward bound from the far off hills,
  And die away, and then grow deathly still.

He gathered grapes upon the hills again;
  Behind old Clinch's peak the sun had waned,
But still he plucked the flowers at Mountain View,
  And from their portals he shook the falling dew.

He heard the bird's wild note as sweet it rang,
  Through the woods so deep from which it sang,
In spring-time he broke the dog-wood bloom,
  And mingled with it the red-bud and cypress broom.

He dreamed that fame had tried to lure his heart
  With every wile, and turn, and magic art,
But from his native home he could not turn,
  And for this humble life ambition spurned.

Amid this dream he saw a winter scene,
  It touched his heart, and made forget the gleam
That hung around his early days and joys,
  Where pleasure's toil alone his thoughts employed.

He saw an aged form, with humble hands
  Let down into an humble grave, while stand
Around a few well-tried and humble friends,
  Who watch the burial rites and last sad end.

He notes the place; it is upon the hill
  Where oft he 'd played and listened to the rill,
Which leaped from rock to rock to reach the vale,
  And wander to the ocean to tell its tale.

Three hours later a friend bent o'er the man,
  And raised the pallid face which looked so grand
And calm, with gas-light streaming brightly o'er,
  He could not cry aloud; he knew no more,

But that he held a corpse upon his arm;
  But the smile so gentle gave no alarm,
Which lingered round the dead man's icy lips,
  For he was dreaming still of sun-set tips,

Upon the peaks around his native home,
  When the vale was not alone, alone,
But loved ones dwelt with him beside the stream,[beam.
  Which flashed and backward gave the moon's soft

This was found upon a scroll beside the dead,
  "Among my native hills my lowly bed
I ask these friends to make, where falling dew
  May drop upon it from trees at Mountain View."

CONCLUSION.

They bore him back to the hills from whence he came,
  Among the trees where oft he 'd cut his name,
And turned the vines into a pleasant swing,
  His body his friends alone had thought to bring,

And let it rest amid these rural scenes.
  Of which joy in dying he had sweetly dreamed;
In dreaming of his early home he smiled,
  And still that smile his friends almost beguiled.

They buried him low where slept his sister's form,
  Again they made them equal, though one forlorn
Had lived and died: and poverty was ever near,
  But still a soul shone noble, pure, and clear.

But high the other had writ his honored name,
  And long the world would let his praises reign,
But who can tell who bore the noblest heart,
  Who was the truest, who need the greatest art!

Though born beneath the same bright star.
  Through life their paths went wide and far.
They met again when death had touched their frames,
  And each for the other's lot had wished the same.

Oh fate! I ask thee which was worst or best,
  Oh! who with the better part was richly blest?
My heart, I leave thee here to choose aright,
  But ever keep thy holy God in sight.

OUR POET-PRIEST.

ON THE DEATH OF FATHER RYAN.

A gentle sigh goes through the land,
  Did you not hear the anguish wild ?
The sound comes to where I stand,
  Borne on breezes from climes so mild,
That every gale is but a breath
Of orange blooms, or sigh of death
    For the gentle soul fled;
Sad earth you know not what is gone,
  Our poet-priest is dead.

Our sighs are heard where chilly winds
  Freeze the April showers to ice,
The land of snow does not rescind
  The swelling tide of love, the price
Of poetry's living stream of thought,
But weeps from hearts with grief o'er fraught,
    For the gentle spirit fled,
The sweet muse of the sunny South,
  Our poet-priest who is dead.

Urania sits with loosened hair,
  And eyes too sad to rain her grief;
Her bosom heaves with dark despair
  Which in her heart now reigns the chief.
Her idle harp swings with the breeze,
The echoing chords with anguish seized.
    Cries, "His spirit has fled
To its eternal home above.
    Our poet-priest is dead."

A seraph bright with sunny locks,
  Sweeps back the awful veil,
To mortal eyes the mystery unlocks,
  And lets us see the soul we wail,
"His harp was tuned with heavenly strings,
Too sweet for earth the song he sings,
    So back his spirit fled
To breathe its music to angels' ears.
    Your poet-priest is dead."

Farewell sweet soul of celestial light,
  Whose song was touched by upper fire !
Me thinks the hand now gone from sight
  Will still awake from that heavenly lyre,
The music grand which wraps us round,
And angels in ecstacy will list the sound.
    But sweet spirit fled.
This will ever echo to our sad hearts,
    Our poet-priest is dead.

———:———

AT THE CLOSE OF 1881.

The old year is slowly, sadly dying,
Soon he must cease on the air to breathe,
The snow on his withered breast is lying,
While the chilly winds o'er him grieve.

A gentle sound from the fairy land
Swells out upon the rising gale,
A soothing touch from an icy hand,
Seems before our minds to sail.

An icy stone from stern memory rolls,
A sepulchral voice whispers there,
"Many have passed to the grave so cold
Who loved you best and dearest here."

THE POET'S GRAVE.

Tread lightly o'er this sacred ground,
For angels fair have kissed the soil,
And with their breath perfumed the mound
That hides the dust from heartless spoil.

Could we but pierce the gloom of death
Where stillness reigns forever more
And scent the lovely flower's sweet breath
That blooms upon that happy shore,

Would we seek the spirit to recall
To earth's dark scenes of toil and woe,
While treasured still in memory's hall
We have the words that charmed us so?

The poet sings his own sad life,
With fevered hands he strikes the chords,
He tells us life is but a sickening strife,
And of creation there are no lords.

"It is madness in my brain
That forces these notes so sad and wild;"
Thus he spoke in fiercest strain,
And in his grief he ceased to be mild.

Poet! sleep on and take thy rest;
Thy broken heart will know no sorrow,
The waves of strife on thy peaceful breast
Are calm, and no storms of to-morrow.

MY LIFE.

Not a single ray of light
  Shines into my lonely heart,
My life has ever been a night
  Into which no sunbeams dart.

My past is a desert waste,
  Where not a flower blooms,
Over which my spirit hastes
  Into a land of darker gloom.

The future! ah! what is my future?
  A wild Plutonian way
Where I alone must wander
  In this dark and cheerless day.

——:——

TO A FRIEND.

On memory's golden harp
I shall try to touch a string,
And wake within your heart,
Music that will forever sing;
Let friendship be the key-note
That it shall echo back to me,
And may the music sweetly float,
Like sun-light on the sea.

THE PHANTOM OF A DREAM.

"Who would love,
Though full of pain, this intellectual being,
These thoughts that wander through eternity,
To perish rather, swallowed up and lost
In the wide womb of uncreated Night,
Devoid of sense and motion?"

—MILTON.

It was a dark and dreary night
When every star was hid from sight,
The wild wind moaned and shrieked around
And filled mine ears with mournful sound,
That dreaming soft of life and death,
How frail our being which is but breath,
I soon forgot the stormy blast,
And frozen rain which kissed so fast
My window pains, but watched the flame
Which from the dying embers came.
It flashed and died but left no blot
That it had burned upon that spot,
Except a dreamy, dusky shade
Which faded almost before 'twas made.
Ah! thus is life, this frail life!
It flames a moment in glorious strife,
Then sinks, but leaving on the earth
A shade of naught that once had birth.
I watched these shades of death with pain,
And by the fancy of my brain,
They grew to human form and face,
And phantoms of other worlds I traced.
The most majestic with noiseless step,
Across the floor in silence swept,
And paused before me grand and tall
Unlike the shadow on the wall;

In hollow voice these words it spoke,
In awful tones the stillness broke,
And every shadow ceased to move,
As if my courage each would prove:
"Enquiring soul, you have asked
The smiles of G)d where angels bask;
The light of truth from His great throne
Who reigns above, and gives alone
To those who wish the words of light;
And here my shade has winged its flight
To bear thee far amid the storm
And crash of worlds, and all alarm,
That round our paths in fury cling,
And from your road the darkness fling.
To you who light and truth have asked,
To me is given the glorious task
Of flinging wide the upper world,
Of showing why poor souls are hurled
Into a chaos of burning zones,
Of showing those who dwell alone,
And wander forth through darkness thick,
With groans of anguish wild and sick,
Of lifting the veil of mystery to you
And the world of spirits let you view."
With quickening breath I started back,
A space of time my brain I racked.
I tried to clasp some object near,
But all seemed barred from me with fear:
Like bird in serpent's magic power,
My fear began to melt and cower,
And soon fast to his dusky wing
I felt myself all boldly cling:
And scarce the window seemed a bar
For through he darted and afar:
I held my breath in awful fear.

While on I fared in darkness drear,
With none to hold and guide my flight,
But this shade from the world of night.
Upon the stormy blast we flew,
But pelting rain could not bedew
The pinions of my gloomy guard,
Nor his mysterious flight retard.
But soon we passed the tearful cloud,
And cut our way through a snowy shroud,
Which round the world hung like a veil;
So thin it was it seemed a sail
Which spirits would set to a phantom ship,
Through soft and sunny waters to dip.
We left the mist and rain behind,
Which seemed the earth with girths to bind;
A dreamy silver light hung o'er
Our lonely globe like magic store.
So rapid was our madening flight,
And dark the awful wings of night,
That soon the earth became a star,
Gleaming softly from afar;
I looked until it faded all away,
And on my sight a glorious day
Had burst, beyond the sight of earth,
Where trembling light a radiant girth
Cast round the rapid course we took.
Dimly lighting up each nook.
A sun we now were sailing by,
A sun so large we saw no sky;
It did not scorch or burn the flesh,
To me a feeling bright and fresh
It gave, as if the flame of life
Within its bosom burned; no strife
Of elements around it rolled,
But rays intoxicating fold

This burning world so radiant with light—
This mass of matter so gloriously bright;
My eyes were blind with near approach,
To ask relief I dared not broach,
Nor would I seek to leave this sphere,
But ever would I dwell so near
That I could feel its reviving fire,
Course through my veins in high desire;
But soon we passed this flaming sun—
Another path the shadow won—
Our road again through darkness lay
And once again we groped our way.
At last a distant star we reached—
A silent, strange, and lonely beach
Which rolled upon the verge of space,
And here alone its orbit traced.
No mortal eye had viewed the sphere,
But to the walls of light so near
Its path in quiet beauty lay,
That from the bright, reflected ray,
Which gleaming fell on gate and wall,
And lit the bright celestial scroll,
Where angels' deeds are sweetly told,
And holy works with truth unfold,
It gained its light; which soft and pale
Now kissed the planets' course so frail.
We paused upon this dreamy globe
Which Heaven itself with rays enrobed;
And on it moved with silent grace,
And flung the darkness from the space
That formed its path; it seemed to move
By love's strong thread, and sure did prove
The power of God, who holds each star,
That rolls and shines in distance far.
And far beyond this lonely sphere,

Which basks in light so heavenly clear,
A thousand worlds seem floating on,
And all seemed near though each alone; [praise,
Through love's sweet balm they sing God's
They tell His glory, and round Him raise
A pyramid of blazing worlds,
Which round His throne by millions whirl;
Like balls of fire they seemed to me,
Which floated through a dark thick sea:
A moment I paused to view this sight,
A moment my heart was filled with light,
Which warmed and thrilled my very soul,
As though an angel fair had told
Of Heaven's beauty, and eternal glory,
A grand, and sweet celestial story.
My phantom guide began to speak,
And unfold the truth which all do seek :
"I bore you to this lonely star
The gates of light and truth to unbar,
From here the shining gates of Heaven,
From which all truth and light are given,
Gleam before your dazzled eye,
And now are free for you to spy.
The skirts of Hell from here are seen,
The land of ice and Lethe's stream.
But first I'll tell my own sad tale,
Though you may weep with woe and wail;
My lot is just—I would not change,
If from my God it would estrange:
Far happier those who know a God,
Though beneath his wrath they are trod,
Than thousands doomed to wander alone,
With hearts to their God as cold as stone.
I ask this boon that you'll not think
That in my heart the darts that sink,

Were sent unjust to rankle there,
And teach my heart to know despair.
·And do not let your soul sink down,
When reasons deep are yet not found.
As raging anguish I describe,
But high with hope your feelings bribe.
I lived in centuries long ago
When God and truth I could not know;
In Grecian Isles called a Sage,
You must know in that glorious age
Of one that justice banished the land,
And then I wept on a foreign strand.
I thought while life and time was mine,
That I had found all truth sublime.
Oh sadest fate ! I knew not then
I had a soul. an immortal gem
Which would shine through crash of worlds;
And systems wrecked that lawless whirl
Through space. will live but as a day,
Ere back they fall to cold decay.
Compared to my eternal soul,
Which will see the centuries roll
But as seconds on your small earth,
And still to it there 'll be no death
Or change to come forevermore,
Upon eternity's bright shore
My life on earth was all to know,
My debt to death was all I owe,
Were thoughts that through my brain did thrill,
And calmed my heart and made grow still
The sad sweet longings that fill each heart.
And from dull reverie madly start,
The dullest. coldest. human life,
And make them long for noblest strife.
These longings come to all mankind,

If he would heed he 'd be not blind.
I tried to make my life so pure,
That highest Gods my name would endure;
And sing my praise on Olympian height,
Where heroes' names alone had right.
And heroes' deeds were all that rung.
And all that Gods on Olympus sung.
My life of fame at last I closed.
And in the earth my dust reposed.
Oh! listen now to what I say,
Mark well my word, I beg, I pray,
A thousand pangs I 've undergone,
For this strange faith and creed alone.
My soul when freed from mortal coil,
Retained the sin of earth's dark soil
Which nature prompted me to do,
As then no better way I knew
To purge my soul I sought the flame,
Which ushered forth without a stain,
From the celestial throne of God eternal,
Who reigns above with laws supernal;
I drank the burning liquid stream,
It thrilled me through and o'er me gleamed,
And all but one, my greatest sin,
Began to fade, and then grew dim,
Until no spot remained to see
Except this one which ever would be.
And this it was—a soul I thought
By God's great hand was never wrought;
And this the flame could not remove,
As constant burning did but prove;
It stung my soul and made me flee
From Heaven's light across this sea
Of gloomy night, which none can tell
Where begins or ends, but hell

On yonder side right closely borders,
From here is heard the fiends' wild orders:
But this is sadest that I can sing,
And this the greatest woe I bring,
Forevermore, as you will see,
The gates of light are closed to me.
But here my soul at certain times,
Must back to Lethe and frozen climes
Be dragged, by a monster grim and dark,
Whose hideous yells and awful bark
Attract the wretch who burns in fire,
And stops his raging pain and ire.
And then my feet in the gloomy tide,
The freezing ice along the side,
Are thrust until it reach my knee,
And then I 'm fixed in this lone sea.
Here I stand till mind and thought
Becomes a blank, and all is naught:
My grim and awful guard with glee
My vacant pulseless soul sets free;
My wings at first refuse to move,
And long I try their power to prove,
I touch the burning brilliant spheres
Which have sung for thousands of years,
Through endless space, of truth and light,
But in my aimless, pathless flight,
I see no worlds, I hear no sound,
I catch no rays—with reverence profound
I try to hear the far off strain,
Which drops from angels' lips, as again
Back and forth through endless night they fly,
Bearing messages from Him on high.
All unconscious I take my way,
While unseen beauties round me play:
I look, but know not what I see,

I try to think, and feel, and be.
A babe I am with senseless mind
Reaching forward and trying to find
An object on which to clasp my hand
By which I may be able to stand.
By slow degrees I gain my strength,
And find unable to reach the length
That once my brain had power to span,
As by the worlds I swiftly fanned,
It seems a century before I gain
·My former thought and lofty frame;
And when 'tis reached what grief to me,
For back I go to oblivions Lethe.
At times I've looked upon the tortured,
And seen their vivid minds, though nurtured
By flames of fire and keenest pain,
And wished their Hell to have my brain.
I've heard the wails of anguish wild,
I've heard the groans from sorrow's child,
I've heard the lost from darkness cry,
As on through eternal night they ply
Their weary way, with longing gaze
Up toward God's throne forever raised;
The sighs of those who knew no fault,
But from the laws of God revolt,
Are sad to hear, and chill the heart,
But ah! my God! what pen or art
Can tell the sorrow I have seen,
When deepest woe has been my dream!
Ah! none to me can I compare,
Nor think they feel my stern despair,
Go teach to mortals what is death—
That life on earth is but a breath;
But in the lump of clay there lives
A deathless soul, which man misgives,

And doubts, and casts beneath his feet.
And makes on earth his life complete.
But ages roll in circles round,
We find no end or commencing ground,
Our souls have been and shall e'er be,
For no shore is found in Eternity."
He ceased and with his shadowy hand
He pointed to our far off strand:
A streak of light still marked our way
Like moon-beams which on the water play,
I tried to raise myself and fly,
My heart was chilled I could but cry,
And forward springing, with a start
I awoke to find the magic art,
The phantom of a troubled dream,
And all things were not what they seemed
Though the fancy of a dream it be,
The phantom's words are more to me.

———:———

ON THE DEATH OF PRESIDENT GARFIELD.

The bells are sadly tolling, tolling,
    The notes of music tell of death;
The human ocean is rolling, rolling,
    And all whisper beneath their breath,
        "Our chief is dead."

Martial sounds are ringing, ringing,
    With a wild funeral knell,
The muffled drum is beating, beating,
    Its last long farewell
            To the chief who is dead.

The nation's tears are flowing, flowing,
  From every heart and eye,
The fire of vengeance is glowing, glowing,
  And vies with that on high,
      For the chief who is dead.

————:————

LIFE AND FATE.

TO A FRIEND.

We are walking together
On the silent dark heather,
With shadows and darkness,
Soft dropping upon us.
From me you are hid,
The gloom my heart chid—
Oh ! the shadows so drear
Kept reaching so near;
But still I am clinging,
While your voice is sweetly singing,
Your face grows whiter
When my burden seems lighter
And we clasp hands in fear
And say ''separate ne'er.''
But so vain is life
That needless is strife,
When comes the great river
That rush and roar forever
It heeds not the cry
That would move the Most High,
But bears the wretch away,
Where darker waters play;
And thus is now our fate,
Before is consummate,
The greatest joy of life,

LIFE AND FATE.

And you become my wife.
The river's surge and foam,
Around forever moan.
Its waters flow between us,
The moon hides in darkness,
The stars give faint their light,
My hopes are hid in night.
I am caught in its tide,
You are left by its side;
My heart cries to thee,
"I am lost in this sea,"
You whisper "I am coming,"
But stop almost in turning.
On angry waves I'm whirled,
I watch the foam madly curl,
My heart grows sick alone,
I try to catch your tone,
But all is lost amid the sound,
That comes from underground,
And angry waters roar,
And sorrow is my store.
Once upon the sea
I catch a sight of thee,
So feeble is the view.
I scarcely know 'tis you.
I wave in mute farewell,
You gave no sign to tell
That we are so near,
Now separated in fear.
I cry aloud to you,
And give my last adieu.
Many years pass away,
Feeble stars alone stray
From behind the gloom.
And struggle in their doom;

·They alone give light.
All else to me is night.
Fame gives a faint smile,
And my heart to beguile
Tries. but all in vain.
For ache will my brain.
But still rush the river.
I on its bosom quiver:
Onward it takes me
To the ocean of Eternity,
There my sail will glide,
But there will be no tide.
You will come soon,
Yes. ere the day is noon,
We will meet again
When the ocean we must stem.
But will our souls know,
Where all perhaps is snow,
That a chord so rang
From our hearts, and sang,
As from an angel's lyre,
Of which no ear could tire ?
I will not lift the veil,
I seek not the tale
Of my future state,
Or what may be my fate.

GUILTY WITHOUT CRIME.

I passed along a rippling stream,
 That rippled like a tear,
And gayly flashed the sun's bright beam,
 Upon each object near;
And as it sung in joy and mirth,
 The cowslip nodded by,
And sweetly kissed the gleeful earth,
 Beneath the butterfly.

Upon one side the little brook
 A restless crowd had pressed,
And with a jealous passion shook
 As some one they addressed;
Across the rivulet they reached, .
 Their victim tried to grasp,
Or sting the soul as loud they preached,
 With hatred's coldest clasp.

A thousand flow'rs grew on the ground,
 The violet so blue,
A lonely clump or pretty mound,
 Had formed in open view;
But no one paused to see the tear
 That sparkled in each eye,
But rudely crushed all blooming near,
 Without a thought or sigh.

The other side the victim stood.
　　A pale and trembling soul.
The body seemed without the blood.
　　And tender was his mold.
And once he bent to pluck a bloom.
　　That touched his aimless feet.
Then stretched his hand to thrust the doom,
　　From off his path so sweet.

A lonely grove came out to view,
　　Upon this meadow side.
The sky above a darker blue,
　　With sun-lit flowers vied.
The morning dew dripped from the trees,
　　Moist was the clinging moss,
Perfume was borne on every breeze.
　　This seemed a heaven to cross.

Around the poet's pallid face,
　　A sun-beam lingered ever.
And o'er each feature you could trace
　　The line of sorrow, which never
Had left the anxious troubled heart,
　　But clung with anguish mild,
As woes that eat and ne'er depart,
　　From sorrow's lonely child.

Upon the flowery shore alone,
　　He trod with trembling step.
And every joy was all his own
　　If here alone he wept.
He kept his face turned toward the wood,
　　As if with ecstacy filled,
And nothing broke his solemn mood,
　　For this our God had willed.

But once he turned and plucked a flower,
  When louder grew the scorn,
Which came in jeering laugh and shower.
  As if they fiends were born.
And as he broke the snowy bloom,
  A tear fell on the leaf,
Which flashed the weary wretched doom
  That must be his in brief.

And near he came to the little stream.
  And meekly stretched his hand,
A sweet sad smile a moment beamed
  Upon the numerous band.
And two or three gave back the smile,
  And seemed to catch the light,
Which played in soft angelic wile
  Across his face so white.

In gentle tones they cheered him on.
  And kindly viewed the flower,
For mercy from them had not gone.
  But fell in a blessing shower;
But ere he caught their well meant sounds,
  The crowd grew wild and rude,
And sought to inflict a deeper wound
  Upon his soul so nude.

But one, with a tender noble thought.
  Had vainly tried to take
The peace-offering the poet had brought.
  For the weary tear's sad sake;
Their fingers met and each turned pale.
  The flower floated down,
The wretched victim wild did wail,
  As down the stream it wound.

GUILTY WITHOUT CRIME.

A moment's time had floated by
    When on the hill I stood,
Looked again upon the sky,
    And the crowd's dark angry mood.
The stream in size had wider grown,
    The people ruder pressed,
The seeds of hate were deeper sown ·
    Down in their burdened breast.

Two friends, with mild and gentle look,
    Came near and yet more near,
They seemed about to cross the brook,
    And dry the poet's tear;
My heart swelled out in gratitude,
    For this was kindness pure,
And not among men the habitude,
    Though often feigned to allure.

The poet came to meet these two.
    A smile upon his lip,
And when he came plainly in view,
    A look of joy had slipped
Into his weary, saddened face,
    And all seemed changed around,
And scarce a line of scorn could trace,
    Nor hear a woeful sound.

But back they turned in trembling fear.
    Before they reached the stream,
The crowd's loud laugh and scoffing sneer
    Had made them shun to dream
A poet's sweet and fevered thought,
    Though colored bright and fair;
With heaven's celestial brightness wrought
    Without a wrong or snare.

The poet turned with wildest woe
    Upon his pallid brow,
To thus be scorned and slighted so,
    And down to shame to bow;
He looked no more across the brook,
    But turned his eye away,
His tender frame with passion shook,
    His anger to betray.

He reached the woods and disappeared
    Beneath the leafy shade,
No more the crowd was to be feared,
    I thought, for he had made
A refuge for his woeful heart,
    And here would rest his soul,
Ne'er at the crowd's rude sneers to start,
    Nor be turned away so cold.

The crowd still sneered and scoffed with hate,
    Though they could not see
The poet's form, and long sedate
    They sat and watched the lea,
The brook, and woods, and far-off trees,
    Filled with sweetest blooms,
While hummed around the honey-bees
    Beneath the shady glooms.

The poet lived in silence deep
    By sweet nature sought,
He scarcely sought a moment's sleep,
    But for his race he wrought:
Into the misty future he saw,
    And read what man should know,
He read the good and the many flaws
    Which would before them show.

He caught the song of wildest bird,
    And told of sweeter sound
By other men which would be heard
    When he should moulder under-ground;
In sweetest strains he touched the soul,
    Of passion yet unknown
He sung in grand and wildest mold,
    And too, of thoughts unsown.

I watched this scene with aching heart,
    Until a rude dark grave
Broke on my sight, and made me start,
    And wildly long to brave
The world's poor scorn and lowly hate,
    And share the wretched lot,
And with the noble poet mate,
    And take each shameful blot.

I begged the crowd to know the stain
    That dragged this soul to woe,
Or what could free, or pardon gain,
    Or joy for him to know.
I could not see why thus they did,
    What wrong had stained his name;
Why did not God on High forbid
    That this should be his fame.

The crowd hissed out in angry tone,
    "Poverty is his sin,
Upon his brow which well is known,
    The stamp is certainly not dim;
He dreams of things which fate should hide
    From every mortal eye,
And God himself will fiercely chide
    The would-be-searcher of the sky.

He thinks to gain a poet's renown,
    To gain a noble honor—
Or wear a gorgerous laurel crown,
    For this we're crushed with horror.
We pray that God will ever curse
    Presumption brought so high,
And every man on earth will nurse
    A sneer and scornful sigh."

An age has passed with flying wing;
    I pass again along,
I hear the brook o'er pebbles sing
    Its sweet and lovely song:
An old man met me by its side.
    And in his hand he bore
A lovely scroll. with gold all tied.
    And read with deepest lore.

He told his tale and this was it.
    Many years ago
A poet passed in musing fit,
    And he had sought to know
Whence and why he came that way:
    Because he could not learn.
He sought to turn his steps astray.
    And deep with scorn he spurned.

The poet died of broken heart.
    And when he found him dead.
And learned to judge of poetic art.
    He turned his mind instead.
Upon the lonely poet's song,
    And found the grandest verse
That does to any work belong:
    But men its source did curse.

GUILTY WITHOUT CRIME.

He told the world both far and wide,
　　He sung his praises loud,
He wrote the poet's name beside
　　The learned and the proud;
He sought the poet's lonely grave—
　　A monument to raise,
That all should know his pains to save,
　　Two names for men to praise.

———— :————

ON THE DEATH OF JOHN T. DAVIS.

Ye who have stood beside the bed,
Caught the last word and sigh,
Ere the loved spirit fled,
Closed the wide starring eye,

Drop for me one only tear,
Yet, let one sigh fill thy breast,
For I will never again fear
Death's destruction or unrest.

I stood alone beside his bed,
I heard the deep sigh of death,
But knew not when his spirit fled,
Nor when the last low breath.

It was whispered, "He is dying,"
But I heard it not nor heeded,
I was only praying, crying,
That I might die when his soul was needed.

Hush ! what is it ?　Why gather
Around the bed on which he lies ?
Must you leave me, dear Brother,
To pain and sorrow that never dies ?

All is over.—How still he lies !.
Can it be he I loved so well ?
Or some cold form of ice
That ne'er will break this awful spell ?

Can he hear me ?   I will call,
And the spirit surely will return;
Oh God! he heeds me not.   All,
My all on earth is gone.

———— :—— —-

"WHO WOULD NOT BE THIS YOUTH ? "

This was said by Cato of old,
Of a bright young boy who died so bold;
As he lay sleeping in death so cold,
He presented a form of beautiful mold.

'Twas said again by Napoleon the great,
As he saw the form of a soldier-mate
Reclining in death,—the warrior's fate,—
And the sun of his life could never set late.

And of our friend it may be said.
Though many hearts for him have bled,
And many tears for him are shed.
As we lay him in his narrow bed.

He gently smiled and passed away,
And still that smile o'er his face did play;
While still in death he sweetly lay,
We scarcely thought his spirit did stray.

His soul will know no bitter wrong.
His tongue be tuned to a heavenly song,
And angels will list the note prolonged,
And around his feet will thickly throng.

Oh ! who would not this sleep partake,
Ere the path of duty he forsake,
Ere shame on his soul a blotch could make,
And to sorrows deep his heart awake ?

Before dark death for duty is rife,
We are saddened and torn by stormy life,
The soul embittered by many a strife,
And we long to end this turbulent life.

———— :————

HIS RETURN.

TO MY BROTHER.

"To-day revenge has been complete,
I quenched the cup of bitter sweet,
And now my heart 's at last replete.

I drank the dying groans of him
Who drugged my life, and made grow dim
My God, and filled up to the brim,

My cup of woe and anguish wild;
On yonder field he was beguiled,
And led to slaughter though a harmless child.

A moment I tried to feel some woe,
And gently make his cruel blood flow,
But who can be mild to a deadly foe ?

To you, my friends, I give my laud,
It was for revenge I joined your band,
But still with you, my friends, I'll stand.

But since I give my native home,
I wish you here to pause alone,
And hear your chieftain's late forlorn.

You, perhaps, have wondered oft,
What fate had tossed me there aloft;
A being with soul, and no part soft.

Come near and let me tell my pain,
With my country's blood my hands are stained,
But shudder not and turn not again.

That I am cursed I would not hide,
When turn you away I will not chide,
But let your pity with me abide.

When I draw nigh you speak in tones
Of whispered breath, and look forlorn,
As if my approach was a sign to mourn.

You oft have marked my evil eye,
My vacant stare, and aimless sigh,
My ever gazing toward the sky.

My rugged hair you too have seen,
The locks that far behind me stream,
Have made a part of my fevered dream.

You oft have marked my pallid brow,
You oft have heard me wildly vow,
A fiend of hell I 'd find, but now,

The task is done.—my heart is still,
No more my veins with fever fill,
No more my soul with passion thrill.

Before thee in my native ground,
To me the bird-note is familiar sound,
And here so oft my bugle I wound.

But those who heard are still and dead,
No more I wake them from their bed,
And every joy for me is fled.

HIS RETURN.

And as I look upon this scene,   •
My soul is wakened as from a dream,
My childhood comes with fancy's gleam.

The breeze that cools my burning cheek,
Has made my soul so wish to seek
My childish joy and early freak,

That I forget to tell my tale,
And let you see the heart that wails,
And against cold fate in anguish rails.

My heart is raised in silent prayer,
When I see the sun's red glare
Upon the mountain top so fair.

For many times I 've climbed its peak,
And caught the eaglets, though a bloody beak
And flapping wings my eye-balls seek.

And once while on this dizzy height,
I saw an eagle and serpent fight,
While high the bird had winged her flight.

When crushed to death she came to die
Where on the cliff her little ones lie,
And close I watched her keep up so high.

When down she fell I scaled the ledge,
And tried, with all my power as pledge,
To unfold the serpent, tight as a wedge.

My heart grew sick to see the fold,
That round the bird the clammy, cold
Snake had drawn, with hatred bold.

Many shades o'er his spiral form
Played, and his fiery eye-balls perform
The sickening work of a fiend born.

But scarcely had I crushed his head,
And tried the eagle, if life had fled,
When then I saw that she was dead.

Oh ! noble sign of my own sad fate,
I could not see until too late,
What would be my future state.

I loved, and it was no common love,
'Twas born of holy thought above,
And settled down like a gentle dove,'

O'er my spirit and made me feel,
With her I loved was the greatest weal,
And no other happiness could be real.

This mad idolatry burned my soul.
And made my thoughts of purer mold,
Like polished metal or refined gold.

Oh let this breeze just fan my face,
And bear my words to the lonely place,
Where sleeps my love, and let her trace,

The bloody course my vengeance took,
Whether I her course basely forsook,
And the wrong allowed my heart to brook.

The gentle lovely being I chose,
Resembled much a muse in repose,
Showed the beauty of the blooming rose.

She gave me all she had for me,
I accepted it with heart full of glee,
But the future I could not see.

And soon I thought to call her mine,
By God's holy law, and right divine,
And with my strength her gentleness twine.

But sudden there came a wondrous change,
A noble lord of manners strange,
Had sought our mountains a month to range.

My lovely Gerald caught his eye,
And long he followed with many a sigh,
And ne'er a moment could I come nigh.

He won her with his flowery words,
He told her tales entirely absurd,
Without a cage he caught my bird.

It was her wish to go I thought,
I dreamed her freedom she had sought,
And set her free, my sweet betrothed!

I did not know the deed I'd done,
I did not think that she I'd won,
I saw no light till set of sun.

For me she loved and not that knave,
My heart and hand was her only crave,
The loss of these drove to the grave.

One stormy night she fled her home;
We knew she did not go alone,
For the stranger left the self-same morn.

I deeply grieved the loss of her,
I grieved in silence without a murmur,
I concealed myself to make no stir.

It was not long till we gained some news,
I deemed her happy under skies of blue,
With her love who would always be true.

For he carried her away to a sunny land,
Where the bright waves dash on the golden sand,
And sun-set gleams all praise demand.

A few short months she was left alone,
Among strangers with hearts as cold as stone,
Who would never heed her grief and moan.

Heart-broken and sick she wandered back,
Begging her way along the track,
With failing strength and courage slack.

She fell at our door one wintry night,
Covered in snow, by the morning light
We found her, breathing slow and slight.

She tried to seek her kindest friend,
And with us came the last sad end,
Where hearts to her every wish would bend.

Dying we all could plainly see,
Her life was stealing away from me,
To leave me alone again to be.

She never knew the friendly hand
Which gave her all she could command,
And ever near would gladly stand.

Her wrongs had stung too deep her heart,
Her mind was a blank, and no kind art
Could dispel the gloom, and knowledge start.

None she knew, but wildly raved,
She told her grief and madly craved
Some kind protection, and to be saved.

I have looked upon a tree decay,
Have heard the war-horse's dying neigh,
Have seen the warrior after a bloody day,

Sleeping placid in his last long rest,
With many wounds upon his breast,
Gaping wide, by none caressed,

The wide-staring eye and cold drawn lip,
Compose the face. and the hair backward slip,
And remove the blood, which fastly dripped:

But what are these to the vacant mind,
Which tries to grasp, but all is blind,
And tries to know what surely is kind.

It was the last night of her life,
Her spirit was passing from all strife,
For death's dark doom I saw she was rife.

The moon streamed in at the open window,
Lit up the room and dying pillow,   [low.
And against the shutter swung the weeping wil-

Each sound that came thrilled mine heart,
Each gust of wind made me start,
For then I felt a woeful part

Had been given for me to act,
And this to me was a bitter fact,
But yet my steps I would not retract.

She called my name in woeful tone,
And with her call there was no moan,
And sweet she spoke without a groan.

God had lent for a little time
Before her death, her vigorous mind,
That she might tell the fate so blind,

Which led away her weary feet,
And gave that fiend a power complete
To crush a life so young and sweet.

My lovely Gerald told her tale,
Without a sigh, without a wail,
She blamed herself and did not fail.

To excuse the sinful wretched deed,
That to this painful death did lead
A pure young heart, and made it bleed.

Within my veins hell then burned,
It would not quench where'ere I turned,
When her sad story that night I learned.

She breathed her last upon my breast.
And sweetly she sunk to her final rest,
And upon her lips a kiss I pressed. -

And with that kiss a vow I made,
A vow that ne'er from my mind could fade,
Unless my hand by death was stayed.

I vowed to roam the wide, wide world.
Where land was found or wave could curl,
Where'er that fiend could hide, and hurl

Dark sneers and taunts at his hateful name,
To drive him mad with bitter shame,
And let him have no right to claim

The justice given to noble men.
And this I swore to do. if send
It did to the grave my every friend.

My soul was seized with hate and blood,
I scarcely knew just where I stood,
So angry was my fiendish mood.

They placed my Gerald in a lonely grave;
For in the church-yard only the saved
Must rest, so said the priestly knave.

I left my home a weary waste,
For kindest friends, in fearful distaste,
Turned from me and mine in haste.

Chilled and cut with such disdain,
I scoffed and spurned their insults plain,
And sought to ne'er see their faces again.

I turned against my native land.
For this was all.—my only plan,
That I could find to dip my hand.

Deep in the blood of the fiendish lord,
Who tried with cruelty's strong chord
To crush, and one more deed to record.

Four long years I've kept my place,
Four long years my steps you've traced,
And always my foe I have faced.

Blood was ever before my mind,
I deemed no subject, but of a bloody kind,
Of sufficient interest for my time.

The more I shed the more I thirsted,
And every wild and cruel burst
I made, my only thought at first,

Was revenge for my great wrong,
And try the fiend's dark agony to prolong,
No matter the time, or how long.

This noble lord knew too well,
That one was on his track as fell
As he, whose revenge he could not quell.

Cruelty long has been my name,
I 've prided myself upon the same,
And never have tried to quench the flame.

Oh! tell me one who has not feared
My noble blade, as fast it neared,
And blanched with horror and eye-ball bleared.

But to-day I 've fought my last,
The wild long note of bugle blast
Will call no more, to try the cast,

Of noble nerve and ringing steel;
My fiery steed with martial peel,
Will never from battle backward reel.

For now we are at rest, peaceful rest,
My warrior steed with death is blest,
And soon the grave my body shall press.

We 've fought together side by side,
And oft his courage with mine has vied,
And never a speer to him I applied.

I sat alone and watched him die,
I heard the last long drawn sigh,
And a tear came in my long dry eye.

Oh saddest fate! that I should tell
My closing deed, which is a knell,
And for my soul rings a passing bell.

When fierce the fight was raging round,
Beneath the war-hoof shook the ground,
And backward came every sound,

My sword was cutting like a reap,
All around the dead lay in heaps,
A youthful warrior forward leaped,

And tried with skillful thrust and true,
To pierce my weary body through,
A task too hard for him to do;

For through his body I passed my blade,
And scarce the rent had I made.
Till his youthful life began to fade.

I glanced into his gentle face,
Oh! God forgive! for there I traced
A familiar look; time and space

Would not suffice to tell my grief,
I thought to seek for him relief,
But well I knew his life was brief.

With pain, the first for years I felt,
Upon the battle-field I knelt,
With saddened heart which could but melt.

And o'er I bent, his dying word
To catch, my soul I tried to gird,
For any tale which would perturb.

He whispered, 'Brother,' and called my name;
A thousand passions through me flamed,
A thousand fiends seem to blame.

It was my youngest little brother,
Who played around the knee of mother,
And scarcely dared to wander further,

Except when I bore him across the hills,
And his heart with joy often filled,
By flowers wild, and laughing rill.

We gathered grapes, and kept the sheep
Till evening shades began to peep,
And to our cot we came to sleep.

I dreamed a moment I was a boy,
My heart all filled with childish joy,
And no crime at my heart to ever cloy.

And when I woke my brother had died,
And I alone by his side,
Remained with heart so sorely tried.

A sweet smile lingered on his lip,
Like sun-set-fades which gently tip,
The far off hills and behind them dip.

I wrapped his country's flag around,
I straightened his limbs upon the ground,
And knelt with heart and soul profound.

I vowed to Him who reigns above,
And governs all with holy love,
To sheath my sword and mailed glove.

And thus you found me, noble friends,
And thus it is my purpose to end,
Oh! help me, comrades, and kindly defend.

There he lies on the silent bier,
And each I ask to drop a tear,
For noble warriors never fear,

This 'll unnerve your manly hearts,
And make you a mark for satire's darts,
To weep when a noble warrior departs.

In yonder vale my love is sleeping,
O'er her grave the willow weeping,
And around the gentle myrtle creeping.

I 'll bear my sacrifice to her lone grave,
And there from God a boon I 'll crave,
To take my soul, and then to save.

When upon the bugle a blast
I blow, and it will be my last,
Your weapons downward quickly caste,

And wend your way across the hill,
Observe good order and be still,
Keep the martial tread and fill,

HIS RETURN.

The fragrant air with war-like sound,
And let it echo all around,
Chiding hill and vale and ground.

I am a warrior and will not weep,
My heart will throb and break and beat,
But still I 'll live through anguish meet.

And when ye reach yon lonely vale
Make no sound of moan or wail,
But approach to learn my tale."

The giant-warrior passed from view,
And in his arms wrapped in blue,
He bore his dead brother through,

The clumpy wood and sighing trees,
Where moans are made by fragrant breeze,
Sufficient to bow the heart and knees.

A few short minutes a bugle blast
Rent the air, and quickly passed,
And forward moved his comrades fast.

With rapid walk they came in sight.
A scene which chilled each heart with fright,
Lay before in the evening light.

Near the grave of her he loved,
The giant warrior had firmly moved,
Still in helmet, breast-plate, and glove.

His mailed hand had done its last,
For through his heart his sword had passed,
While kind and loving his brother he clasped.

The sacred dead was buried alone,
By comrades' hands, while gently moan
The summer breeze, with fragrance blown.

A HUMAN HEART IN THE SKY.

We had wandered alone to the green hill side,
  At the distant mountains we gazed afar,
We had watched the clouds each other chide,
  And flash with lightning as a brilliant star;
We talked of love and the human heart,
We spoke of our lots, and each other's part.

My heart was cold and I could not see,
  My thoughts had wandered to other climes,
I dreamed of a far off sun-lit sea,
  Where heavenly music always chimes;
I dreamed not that a world lay just around,
A world of music and celestial sound.

I watched the clouds in dreamy delight,
  I watched each flash from their gauzy breast,
And peaks stood out like mountains bright,
  And in living lightning themselves they dressed;
Nor were the clouds of gloomy darkness,
But some now looked the moon's soft whiteness.

My friend's soft tones just touched mine ear,
  I heard his voice as from a distance borne,
And his accent sounded strangely clear,
  And made me think him sad and forlorn,
I tried to turn my heart in pity,
And draw my thoughts from my silent city.

When back I turned to the brilliant sky,
  A change had touched this shadowy world,
The many clouds had floated by,
  And on by the gentle winds were whirled;
But just above my favorite hill,
A human heart stood deathly still.

And over its snowy folds there flashed
  A sheet of lightning, like human blood,
As through the veins the warm streams dash,
  And back to the heart the reddening flood;
My heart stood still in wild affright,
For God. I thought, had wrought this sight.

As still it gleamed and reddened more,
  And a thousand brilliant lights gave out,
I dreamed that passion was the store,
  That o'er this heart and all about
Now flashed, and trembled till it seemed alive,
And this living emblem my heart revived.

I turned to look upon my friend,
  He saw the change and blessed the cloud,
I knew my future lot and end,
  And kind and gently spoke aloud,
I could not crush a human heart,
Which burned with passion in every part.

The cloud a lesson to me had taught,
  While fiery lightning o'er us played,
Its burning breast a work had wrought,
  And from a wrong my soul had stayed;
For who could touch a noble soul,
If all its woes were kindly told?

THE PILGRIM TO ETERNITY.

The night was dark, and chill, and dreary,
The wind was blowing, and ne'er grew weary,
The snow fell fast upon the ground,
And clothed the earth. that it made not a sound
As foot-steps fell upon the street,
Of passers-by who sought retreat,
From storm and snow and wintry rain,
The chilly night the beggar restrained,
As he slunk away to his wretched den,
He left the pence for another to glean.
The wealthy merchant, beneath the lamp
Paused a moment, to shake off the damp
Of snow and rain, and button tight
His warm fur-coat, which gleamed so bright.
The light gleamed brighter than pen can tell,
And fell with a glare remarkably well,
Upon the front of a great stone-wall,
Which enclosed a house with gables tall.
And gorgeously gleamed the hall inside,
As gas-light flames with each other vied;
The passer-by would stop and gaze,
Upon the scene which brightly blazed;
Through rooms with marble pillars and stands,
Where shone the richness of every land,
Fair ladies swept in silken robes,
Whose texture seemed from other globes;

And jewels rich reflected bright
And gave the scene a double light;

THE PILGRIM TO ETERNITY.

The gallants swarmed where the fairest sat,
And paid their flattery. and all of that
Which soothes the heart of women fair,
And makes them with each other compare.
And softest music floated around,
Except at intervals, when the sound
Grew loud and full, like shouts of joy,
And every nerve and heart employ;
Again it swelled like a pean of glory,
To a martial chief, with hands all gory,
Or a wild, plaintive, tearful strain;
And then the sound came floating by,
Which roused the quest, and made them vie
In graceful step and movement soft,
As fast they floated round and oft.
Bright flowers mingled with this scene,
The richest hues with evergreens,
Around marble-pillars twined,
Or a cozy nook beautifully lined;
Marble fountains splashed with water,
And sweet perfume floated nearer,
As the spray in diamond beads
Fell around like Heaven's mead.
Bright joy sparkled in every eye,
The spirits of all were running high ;
'Tis sweet to feel this thrilling gladness,
Before the heart is wrung with sadness;
'Tis sweet to steal an hour from care,
Where joy is uppermost without a snare;
But ah ! how sad, when heart is cold,
And never again a joy will behold,
How sad to see a soul so dead,
That all upon it sinks like lead;
But such a scene as this bright place
Could rouse the saddest, and leave no trace

Of deepest woe, and deepest grief,
Though the joy would be so brief.
But sudden there came a gust of air
That chilled the gallant and the fair,
And none could tell from whence it came,
Or why grew faint the radiant flame,
Which sparkled o'er the gorgeous scene,
And gave each object a sickly gleam;
Before a moment could pass away,
Ere the heart could conquer all dismay,
A figure strange stood in their midst,
And destroyed each guest's strong wits.
The form was tender with youthful mold,
But the face was prematurely old,
And backward streamed the dusky locks,
Moist with rain and snow, which mocked,
In pallor his wan white face,
Where lines of sorrow you could trace;
The eyes, of warmest, darkest shade,
The deepest wildest purpose portrayed;
A thrill of horror ran through each frame,
Each breath they drew came hard with pain,
The music died in jarring sound,
And the echoes clashed all around,
The guest stood still, though half the dance
Was finished, and all with startled glance
Looked upon this strange and weird form,
Who like a startled bird in storm,
Had fled into this gorgeous light,
And scared them all to wild affright;
The wild-eyed visitor moved his hand,
And muttered low in tones of command,
"Peace ! Be still, my stranger friends,
And hear what life to you must lend:"

With pallid cheek they all came near,
As if spell-bound. they stood in fear,
And held their breath to hear his word,
Each felt the blood in their veins curd;
All joyous thought had fled the breast,
And doubt upon each bosom pressed;
He spoke and all grew deathly still,
For each with his words were strangely thrilled,
"I am called the pilgrim to Eternity,
But all our steps go to that silent sea,
And few this fact can recognize,
We think of what only is before our eyes,
And dream not of the visions bright,
Which would give to our path a brilliant light.
My God once blessed my burdened soul,
And made it change to a goodly mold,
He gave me visions of future events,
And gave to my heart welcome contents,
Shapes of woe and joy passed by,
Some far off, some so nigh;
I pass through crowds and turn not aside,
For oh! my God with me abides,
I hear their worldly tones and talks,
But still right on the pilgrim walks;
I seek the stranger to tell my tale,
I go to those to whom it will avail
Some future good, and let them know
That all of life is not a woe,
So list while I my story tell,
And then to you I'll bid farewell.
There is a force in the mind of man,
An inward working that can span
With one brief bound, the shadowy past,
And read the future by its cast.
The soul can hush the noise of earth,

Of what may be the future's birth,
And stand alone on the shore of time,
With eager ears may catch the chime
Of ages past; and distant sound.
As murmurings far they fly around,
May touch with echoes low and drear,
A chord that wakes an endless fear,
This chord will whisper, in murmurs low,
The future lot of man below,
Will paint the sky of darkest hue,
Along the shore will thickly strew
The gloomiest wrecks that man can see,
And leave no spot for a sun-lit lea;
This vision cold will chill the heart,
The soul will look for no better part,
The past will be a gloomy waste,
The future too dark for man to taste.
'Twas thus I stood forgetting all
My future dreams and bliss so small,
Oblivious to the earth, my soul
Was wrapped in vision's wildest mold;
I thought I stood upon a height,
And time lay free before my sight,
Where I could view the deeds of guilt,
And drops of grief from wronged hearts spilt.
Me thought the past and future met
Upon a shore, where walked and wept
The many thousands, who move in life,
And seemed to be in endless strife,
Like waves from angry ocean's breast,
Which lash the coast in mad unrest,
The past, with gloomy angry waves,
Cast up her dead from ancient graves;
And there they lay amid the living,
Or back into the waters rolling.

To float and quiver with the motion
Of the wrecks of all that dread ocean.
My heart grew sick to see each take
The shadow of what in life they forsake.
When death closes o'er their weary eye,
And the shades of eternity draw nigh.
Sometimes the bodies float in blood,
An army all in one red flood;
Then on a sea all thick with dust,
Lay those who many ages must
Have lived in fame and glory's beam,
For round them played a dazzling stream;
Others where flashed unearthly light
In lurid flames. and changed the night
Into a wearied unholy day,
Betrayed the poet's frenzied lay,
Here still within his feverish brain,
Burned the zeal and ached the pain,
That touched his pen with passion's fire,
And made him strive with heavenly ire.
But many lay without a tide,
Who knew not what was love or pride;
It was a thick dark stagnant sea
That raised these sluggish corpses to me.
A thousand wrecks lay on the sands,
Of those who dropped almost in bands;
But o'er their forms the living walk,
Nor paused a moment in their anxious talk,
To see the fate of their fellow friend,
Who had reached life's great end;
And some there were who did not care,
But walking on, they did not spare,
Nor fear to spurn, in their great speed,
The corpse which cloy their way, and freed

From every bar, they strain their eyes
Upon the sea where now expires;
But some bent o'er the ashy dead,
And ere the life from them had fled,
They tore from off their bodies the gems,
And jewels bright, and diadems.
I watched the living as they moved,
And to my eyes they quickly proved,
That foul disease was in their frames,
And naught could quench these fearful flames;
They jostled each other, and trampled the weak,
And none in their walk would try to be meek;
Each with hatred watched the other,
And none among them seemed to be brother.
A sky hung o'er this awful scene,
More horrid, terrible, than a dream,
A thunder-cloud upon the sea,
With spots like blood and fire, that to me
Seemed spreading wide, to o'er-cast the sky,
Over the land and round me nigh.
Contracting then almost from view
It passed, like stars discovered new.
When thus gone out and faded away,
The stormy cloud grew bright as day,
And lit the scene with a brilliant blaze,
That scarce the eye could stand to gaze.
It melted then into a dreamy light
Of gold and purple hue, and quite
O'er-spread the shore, and gave a glow,
A ghastly glow, to all below.
I stood listening to the muttering moan
Which echoed through my heart alone,
I stood gazing upon these gleams
Of blood, and light, and sickly beams,
Till sick with fear I turned away,

But could not go, or do else but stay;
I wished to stand forever more,
Where past and future become one shore.
The horror that lay so plain to view,
Filled with awe, but still it drew
My bewildered soul and brain,
And then fascination's wildest strain;
When through me ran, like streams of fire
The burning thought, that on this pyre
I too must lie a victim cold,
And float as those a century old;
Again I turned with scorching fear,
And tried to pierce my future near;
Tried to read my future doom,
If my soul would find aught but gloom
If these dreads that turn the brain,
Would leave me free from every pain;
But all in gloomy stillness slept,
Except where here and there had swept
A ray reflected from the past,
Which quivered, sunk, and died at last.
Me thought to plunge beneath the flood
And end my dread just where I stood;
To meet the future, where is change,
Where still must be no action strange,
But all the same dark, lurid hue.
And sweat from centuries gone, bedew
The brow of those who labor here,
Was more than I in doubt could fear.
But scarce had these my bosom shook,
And tore with grief I could not brook,
When like a dream from Heaven there came
A stream of light, and brilliant flame,
And in its path a being so bright,
That fled the darkest shades of night,

Swept down before my aching brain,
And turned my thoughts away from pain.
His hair streamed back in a gentle breeze,
That fanned a brow which well might please
The loftiest seraph that dwells above,
And serves the God of everlasting love;
A light played o'er his angelic face,
And there my eyes could easily trace
The heavenly thought and spotless heart,
Which from my soul drew with a start,
A strain of music, soft and sweet,
Which thrilled with pain and made complete,
The revolution in my mind,
And ope my eyes which were so blind.
Cold drops of sweat stood on my brow,
My lips were white with fear; but now
I stood entranced, but could not speak,
Nor move my hands, so cold and weak,
But not with fear, for that had fled,
And left me with this vision fed.
He paused, he ceased his rapid flight,
And fanned me with his wings of light;
Into my soul he looked with eyes
That drew, yet burned with magic fires,
I sought to view the sea again,
Where all the past before had been,
But lo! a cloud of darkness thick,
Had o'er-spread the waves so quick,
That not a spot could now be seen,
And night hung o'er, a dusky queen.
I turned my eyes upon the shore,
That, too, had fled forevermore.
What force had hid these views from me,
I could not learn, I could not see,
But this I knew—my heart was warm,

No longer my breast shook with alarm.
With quivering lip I tried to ask,
'Bright seraph, who long hast basked
In Heaven's celestial rays, I beg
From Mercy's cup though naught but dregs
There be, one drop to cool my soul,
For long hath love and hope been cold.'
He moved his wand, and whispered low,
'Look!' and like a radiant bow,
Each motion of his hand had left
A streak of light, a glittering cleft,
Where darkness long the future hid,
And long my forward steps forbid.
It rolled away like fog and mist,
Before the sun, when soft he kissed
The maiden brow of lovely morn,
Ere fragrant dew had dropped in scorn.
Before me lay a scene—ah! a scene,
That well might be a fantastic dream,
A long rough road with jagged storms,
On which men sat with tears and groans,
A flower or two on the side,
Bloomed in loneliness and pride,
But gave no beauty to the way
Though their shades were borrowed from day;
A grassy plot came out to sight,
And to the path looked so bright.
Myself I saw upon this road,
While down the human stream flowed,
Though weary I looked, my heart was free
From every pain, and I bowed my knee,
To Him who reigns and loves us well.
I tried His deeds to do, and tell
His law to all who near me came,
And some noble thought to name,

These voices came in thunder strains,
And seemed to wake my heart and brain;
An aged man with snowy hair,
And tearful eyes, which looked despair,
Had sought my face and seemed to say,
'Help, my child, I beg, I pray!'
An orphan beckoned with his hand,
And tried upon his feet to stand;
A beggar whispered, 'Give me bread,
Or soon I must be with the dead!'
'Whate'er thy lot may be, faint not,
Go, do thy part, though dark thy lot,'
The angel said, and left me here
To feed the poor, to dry the tear
Of those who weep upon the shore,
Where Time, Eternity, forevermore,
Has sent a shade like murky night,
To bar us from the future's light.''
The stranger ceased and turned away,
And left this bright artificial day;
The guest stood mute in wild despair,
And each upon the other would stare,
But roused at last they turned in haste,
And left the halls a dreary waste,
Each guest felt for years to come,
That some great power had struck them home,
Ennobled the heart, and purged the soul,
And changed their thoughts to a holy mold.

FINIS.

INDEX.

www.ingramcontent.com/pod-product-compliance
Lightning Source LLC
Chambersburg PA
CBHW020233090426
42735CB00010B/1681